C29 0000 0723 713

D0539546

Published in Great Britain in 2015 by Wayland
First published in 2008

Text copyright © Pat Thomas 2015
Illustrations copyright © Lesley Harker 2015

Dewey number: 617.6
ISBN: 9780750294294
10 9 8 7 6 5 4 3 2 1

Wayland, an imprint of Hachette Children's Group
Part of Hodder & Stoughton
Carmelite House, 50 Victoria Embankment
London EC4Y 0DZ

Wayland Australia
Level 17/207 Kent Street
Sydney, NSW 2000

Concept design: Kate Buxton
Series design: Elaine Wilkinson

Printed in China

An Hachette UK Company

www.hachette.co.uk

www.hachettechildrens.co.uk

Do I Have to Go to the Dentist?

A FIRST LOOK AT HEALTHY TEETH

PAT THOMAS
ILLUSTRATED BY LESLEY HARKER

WAYLAND

Before you brush your teeth tonight, think about all the things you couldn't do if they weren't there.

Without your teeth you couldn't
sing or smile or speak clearly,
or bite into a crunchy apple.
You couldn't make funny faces.
It would be hard to pretend
to be a snarling dog or
a roaring lion.

That's why it's important to look after your teeth. And most of the time it's easy to take care of them yourself.

You can do this by not eating
sweet or sticky snacks and
drinks. Also make sure
you brush your teeth
really well after
meals and before
you go to bed.

But sometimes it's good to have a little extra help with taking care of ourselves.

The person who helps us to take care of our teeth
is a special kind of doctor called a dentist.

What about you?

Can you think of other people who help us take care of ourselves?

How do they help us?

Why do you think we need their help?

If you have never been to the dentist
you may wonder what it will be like.

Some of your friends or family may have teased you or told you scary stories about going to the dentist. This might make you feel worried.

But no one should feel
worried about going
to the dentist.

Your dentist is there to help take care of you.
Your parents or carers trust him or her and
you can, too.

What about you?

What do you know about dentists?

Who do you know who visits a dentist?

What have they told you?

Most dentists' offices are busy.
Sometimes you have to wait
before you can be seen.
But usually there are
toys and books.

When it's your turn you'll be taken into a room with a big chair that goes up and down. There will also be equipment like special brushes and a big bright light to help the dentist see inside your mouth.

You'll wear a big bib that keeps your clothes clean. Even grown ups wear this.

Your dentist will check that your teeth are clean and that new teeth are growing straight. A check will also be made for any cavities, or holes, in your teeth.

At every visit your dentist will also give
your teeth a really good clean with an
electric brush and polishing paste.

It's a bit noisy and it tickles
a little as it whizzes around
your mouth, but it leaves
your teeth smooth
and shiny.

A cavity is caused by germs and bits of food
left on your teeth if you don't brush properly.

The cavity can get bigger and deeper and
become painful if it isn't fixed.

To fix a cavity, the dentist may take a
special picture of your tooth called
an x-ray to see how deep it is.

If you have a cavity, your dentist will clear away damaged bits of tooth with a tiny drill. The hole is then repaired with a special mixture called a filling.

You will have an injection of medicine so you won't feel the drill. This might sting for a second but soon you won't feel anything in your mouth – at least for a while.

Your teeth aren't just for smiling – or snarling. They also help you chew so you get all the goodness out of your food. So when your teeth are healthy the rest of you is, too.

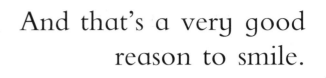

And that's a very good
reason to smile.

HOW TO USE THIS BOOK

Going to the dentist is one of life's necessities. It may not always be fun but neither does it have to be traumatic. The best way to help your child appreciate the importance of going to the dentist is to get him or her used to it from an early age. Early check-ups are usually quick and easy and help your child to get used to what a dentist's surgery looks, sounds and smells like. It also ensures that your child gets into the routine of getting their teeth checked regularly early in life, and may well help to identify and minimize tooth problems.

Most children who are anxious about visiting the dentist, pick up their parents dental anxieties, so wherever possible lead by example. Even before your child is ready to go to the dentist you can take him or her along on one of your own appointments. With some children it may help if there is another adult with you to look after your child whilst you're having a check-up. This allows your child to observe what's going on. Even if you are not totally comfortable at the dentist, it is important to put on a calm and relaxed face – one that portrays a dental check as a normal part of life.

In the same vein, don't let your friends or the child's siblings scare your child with stories about their own 'bad' experiences with a dentist. Watch your language when your child is at the dentist; avoid using words like 'hurt' or 'pain' or 'brave'.

Despite the myths and scare stories that children may hear from friends and family, most dentists are friendly, competent and not at all scary. However, it is important that your dentist is skilled at working with children and understands your child's needs (for instance if your child wishes to have you there during examinations). If you or your child is not happy with a particular dentist – even one you have been going to for years – find another one that suits your child better.

Never use a visit to the dentist as a threat to get your child to avoid sweets or take care of his or her teeth. Instead, set a good example by eating well yourself and brushing your own teeth after eating and before going to bed. With very young children, always supervise brushing to make sure it is done properly.

Play dentist with your children. Check teddy's teeth for cavities (use a toy camera to take an x-ray); teach dolls (or dinosaurs) to brush properly. All these things will help familiarize your child with taking care of themselves and the kinds of procedures they may be exposed to in a dentist's office.

The importance of caring for teeth and gums is part of every school health curriculum from a very early age. However schools can help familiarize children with going to the dentist by arranging visits from practitioners in the local community. They can talk to children about the importance of good oral health and how dentists contribute to it. Such visits can certainly help children cope better when they do have to go to the dentist.

BOOKS TO READ

Open Wide: My first Trip to the Dentist
Jen Green and Mike Gordon (Wayland, 2007)

My First Visit to the Dentist
Monica Hughes and Angela Royston (Heinemann, 2003)

Why Should I Brush my Teeth?
Louise Spilsbury (Heinemann, 2004)

Going to the Dentist
Anne Civardi (Usborne, 2005)

A Visit to the Dentist
Paul Humphrey (Watts, 2007)

RESOURCES FOR ADULTS

British Dental Health Foundation
Smile House
2 East Union Street
Rugby
Warwickshire CV22 6AJ
Tel: 0870 770 4000
Helpline: 0845 063 1188
Web: www.dentalhealth.org.uk

British Dental Association
64 Wimpole Street
London W1G 8YS
Tel: 020 7935 0875
Web: www.bda.org